The Loch Ness Monster

by Jacqueline Laks Gorman

Gareth Stevens Publishing
A WORLD ALMANAC EDUCATION GROUP COMPANY

j 001.94
GoR

Please visit our web site at: **www.garethstevens.com**
For a free color catalog describing Gareth Stevens Publishing's
list of high-quality books and multimedia programs,
call 1-800-542-2595 (USA) or 1-800-387-3178 (Canada).
Gareth Stevens Publishing's fax: (414) 332-3567.

Library of Congress Cataloging-in-Publication Data

Gorman, Jacqueline Laks, 1955-
    The Loch Ness monster / by Jacqueline Laks Gorman.
        p. cm. — (X science: an imagination library series)
    Includes bibliographical references and index.
    Summary: An introduction to the creature known as the Loch Ness monster,
describing efforts to identify and document this phenomenon.
    ISBN 0-8368-3200-0 (lib. bdg.)
    1. Loch Ness monster—Juvenile literature. [1. Loch Ness monster. 2. Monsters.]
I. Title. II. Series.
QL89.2.L6G67 2002
001.944—dc21   2002022516

First published in 2002 by
Gareth Stevens Publishing
A World Almanac Education Group Company
330 West Olive Street, Suite 100
Milwaukee, WI 53212 USA

Text: Jacqueline Laks Gorman
Cover design and page layout: Tammy Gruenewald
Series editor: Betsy Rasmussen
Picture Researcher: Diane Laska-Swanke

Photo credits: Cover, pp. 7, 9, 11 © Fortean Picture Library; p. 5 © Joe McDonald/Visuals
Unlimited; p. 13 © Ivor Newby/Fortean Picture Library; p. 15 © Nicholas Witchell/Fortean
Picture Library; p. 17 © Bettmann/CORBIS; p. 19 © Loren Coleman/Fortean Picture Library;
p. 21 © Tony Healy/Fortean Picture Library

Printed in the United States of America

1 2 3 4 5 6 7 8 9 06 05 04 03 02

Front cover: A man named Anthony Shiels says
he took this picture of the Loch Ness Monster in
1977. Some people think that the picture is a fake.

TABLE OF CONTENTS

Words that appear in the glossary are printed in **boldface** type the first time they occur in the text.

THE BEAST IN LOCH NESS

Some people say something strange lives in the middle of **Loch** Ness. They say it has a large body, a small head, and a long neck. They say it has humps, flippers, and small front legs. People call it "Nessie."

Loch Ness is a long lake in Scotland. The lake is very deep, almost 1,000 feet (305 meters) in some places. The water is dark, foggy, and very cold, but it never freezes. This lake has fish and plants, but no other animal life.

Long ago, the lake was attached to the sea. Maybe a **prehistoric** beast somehow got caught in the lake. Maybe the beast's relatives still live in the lake today.

The ruins of Urquhart Castle are next to Loch Ness. This area of Scotland is very beautiful. Many people visit each year, hoping to see Nessie.

LEGENDS OF LAKE MONSTERS

People have always told stories about sea monsters. Long ago, **Viking** ships displayed statues of dragons or sea serpents. The boats themselves were often shaped like sea monsters. The Vikings also told legends about a terrible sea beast called the "kraken."

The oldest story about the Loch Ness Monster is from the year 565. An Irish **monk** saw a giant water beast. The beast was attacking a swimmer, and the monk drove it away.

Other lakes may have monsters, too. Some people believe a creature called Champ lives in Lake Champlain, between New York and Vermont. Some others believe a creature called Ogopogo lives in Lake Okanagan, in Canada.

In an old picture from Norway, a sea serpent attacks a ship. Many people around the world tell legends and stories about such powerful creatures.

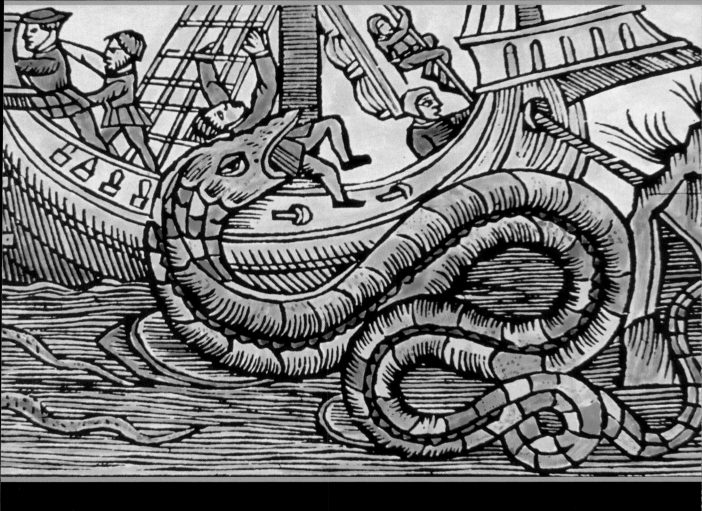

THE LEGEND GROWS

In 1933, a new road was built along Loch Ness. Many more people could now see the lake. Building the road also made a lot of noise, which may have disturbed Nessie, because there were many sightings of the monster after this.

Later, two people were driving along that road and saw a giant creature with two humps. The beast walked along in front of them and then went into the water.

Later that year, a farmer named Hugh Gray saw something in the lake. Gray took a picture of it. It looked like something was swimming just under the water's surface.

This is the picture taken by Hugh Gray in 1933. It is supposed to be the first picture ever taken of the monster. Or does it just show ripples on top of the lake?

PHONY FOOTPRINTS AND PHOTO

A **big-game** hunter named Marmaduke Wetherell was hired to find Nessie in late 1933. Wetherell discovered four big footprints, but they turned out to be fake. Someone had made the footprints using a stuffed hippopotamus's foot.

The next year, a doctor named Robert Kenneth Wilson showed everyone a picture he took of Nessie. The picture became famous and was called the "surgeon's photograph."

There was only one problem. In 1994, a newspaper printed a story about Marmaduke Wetherell's step-grandson. The step-grandson confessed that the picture was a fake and that Dr. Wilson was involved in the **scam**.

The famous "surgeon's photograph" was taken in 1934. Later, a man admitted that it was really a picture of a model attached to a toy submarine.

RESEARCHERS TRY TO FIND NESSIE

A Nessie **craze** began. Many people said they saw Nessie. People tried to prove Nessie was real. One "Nessie hunter," Tim Dinsdale, spent a week watching Loch Ness in 1960. Dinsdale said he was able to film the monster, but the film was not very clear. Some people thought the film showed only a motorboat.

Scientists tried different ways to find Nessie. In 1963, scientists set off explosives to try to upset the beast. In 1968, scientists used sonar equipment to see if there was anything under the water. Sonar sends out sound waves, which bounce back if they hit big things. The scientists got three sonar **echoes** of a large object moving fast near the bottom of Loch Ness.

Tim Dinsdale spent years looking for Nessie. He said he saw her twice after 1960 but did not have his camera with him. This picture shows him on Loch Ness in 1969.

UNDERSEA PICTURES

In the 1970s, scientists from the American Academy of Applied Science tried to find Nessie. The scientists used sonar to map the bottom of the lake. Then they used special cameras and equipment to photograph under the water.

The scientists took four underwater pictures that seemed to show Nessie. Computers were used to make the pictures clearer. Two of the pictures seemed to show a large flipper. Another picture seemed to show a big body with a head, neck, and flippers. The last picture seemed to show a head and face.

Some people said the pictures might show an object, not a living animal.

Dr. Robert Rines is head of the American Academy of Applied Science. He has been looking for Nessie for thirty years. He is shown here adjusting an underwater camera.

DOUBTING SCIENTISTS

Does the Loch Ness Monster exist? Many scientists do not think so. These scientists say people can mistake many things for Nessie, such as driftwood, tree trunks, dead plants, shadows, reflections, ripples, and waves left by boats. A mist over Loch Ness often confuses people, too.

Some people want proof that Nessie is real. These people want someone to catch a live monster or find the body of a dead one. These same people also want to know why, if Nessie really exists, no one has ever found a skeleton or **fossil** of this kind of beast.

Some people say that the dark area at the bottom of the picture is the Loch Ness Monster. It could be other things as well, such as pieces of dead plants.

WHAT COULD NESSIE BE?

If Nessie is real, what kind of animal is it? One guess is that Nessie is a plesiosaur. Plesiosaurs were huge **reptiles** that lived in the sea. These reptiles became **extinct** 70 million years ago, but maybe some plesiosaurs somehow survived in Loch Ness.

Other ideas are that Nessie is a giant salamander, a huge eel, or a giant sea slug, but these animals all look very different from Nessie. Some people think Nessie might be a giant turtle, or some kind of **mammal**, like a whale, porpoise, or sea cow. There are reasons that make these ideas unlikely as well.

Maybe Nessie is a completely new animal that scientists do not yet know about.

Plesiosaurs were fish-eating reptiles that once swam in the seas around Scotland. They grew fifty feet (15 m) long. Like Nessie, they had small heads, large bodies, flippers, and long necks.

THE SEARCH GOES ON

The search for Nessie is not over yet. Scientists are still using high-technology equipment and sonar to study the lake. The scientists have found huge objects moving deep in the water, but they still have not proved anything.

Dr. Robert Rines and his team from the American Academy of Applied Science went back to the lake in 1997, 1998, and 2001. The team put sonar, lights, and video cameras underwater. The equipment runs all the time, and people can view pictures from Loch Ness over the Internet.

Many people want to know if Nessie is out there.

People are still looking for the Loch Ness Monster. Researcher Steve Feltham, a "Nessie hunter," is shown ready to photograph anything interesting on Loch Ness.

MORE TO READ AND VIEW

Books (Nonfiction)   *Beastly Tales: Yeti, Bigfoot, and the Loch Ness Monster. Eyewitness Readers* (series). Malcolm Yorke (DK Publishing)

The Loch Ness Monster. Mysteries of Science (series). Elaine Landau (Millbrook Press)

Mystery of the Loch Ness Monster. Can Science Solve (series). Holly Wallace (Heineman Library)

Scary Science: The Truth Behind Vampires, Witches, UFOs, Ghosts and More! Sylvia Funston (Owl Books)

Books (Fiction)   *The Boggart and the Monster.* Susan Cooper (Margaret McElderry Books)

Little Nessie. Julia Mowery (Dobie Book Publishing)

Monsters Don't Scuba Dive. Adventures of the Bailey School Kids (series). Debbie Dadey and Marcia Thornton Jones (Little Apple)

Sea Monsters Don't Ride Motorcycles. Adventures of the Bailey School Kids (series). Debbie Dadey and Marcia Thornton Jones (Little Apple)

The Water Horse. Dick King-Smith (Crown Publishing)

Videos (Nonfiction)   *Ancient Mysteries: The Loch Ness Monster.* (A&E)

The Beast of Loch Ness. (NOVA)

Loch Ness Discovered. (Discovery Channel)

Videos (Fiction)   *In Search of History: Loch Ness Monster.* (A&E)

Loch Ness. (MGM/UA Video)

Secret of the Loch. (Just for Kids Home Video)

Shelley Duvall's Bedtime Stories, Volume 3: Little Toot and the Loch Ness. (Universal Studios)

22

WEB SITES

Web sites change frequently, but we believe the following web sites are going to last. You can also use good search engines, such as **Yahooligans! [www.yahooligans.com]** or **Google [www.google.com]** to find more information about the Loch Ness Monster. Some keywords that will help you are: *Loch Ness, Loch Ness Monster, cryptozoology, sea monsters,* and *Nessie.*

www.ajkids.com

Ask Jeeves Kids, the junior Ask Jeeves site, is a great place to do research. Try asking:

What is the Loch Ness Monster?

Are there lake monsters?

Or, just type in words and phrases with "?" at the end, such as:

Loch Ness?

Nessie?

www.yahooligans.com

This junior version of the Yahoo site is very easy to use. Simply type in the words "Loch Ness monster" to get a list of sites that are appropriate for kids.

www.unmuseum.org

The *Museum of Unnatural Mystery* is an online museum of strange things. The "Lost Worlds Exhibition" allows you to read about cryptozoology, the study of creatures that are not proven to exist.

www.cryptozoology.com

Devoted to the study of unseen animals, the *Cryptozoology* site has information on Nessie and other interesting beasts from around the world.

www.nessie.co.uk

This *Legend of Nessie* web site contains up-to-date information about studies and expeditions, reports of encounters, photos, sketches, and more.

www.simegen.com/writers/nessie/index.html

This site, called *Nessie's Grotto*, has a newsletter, interviews with eyewitnesses and researchers, games, and a puzzle.

www.pbs.org/wgbh/nova/lochness

This companion site for the *NOVA* television show has information on the legend of Loch Ness, other fantastic creatures, eyewitness accounts, and sonar experiments.

GLOSSARY

You can find these words on the pages listed. Reading a word in a sentence helps you understand it even better.

big-game (BIHG GAYM) — large animals hunted for sport. 10

craze (KRAYZ) — something people become excited, or crazy, about for a time. 12

echoes (EH-kohs) — sounds that repeat after bouncing off a surface. 12

extinct (eks-TEENKT) — no more of a species left alive. 18

fossil (FAHSS-uhl) — the remains of a plant or animal that lived long ago. 16

loch (LAHK) — the Scottish word for lake. 4, 6, 8, 12, 16, 18, 20

mammal (MAM-uhl) — a hair-covered, warm-blooded animal, that nurses its young. 18

monk (MUNK) — a man of a certain religion that lives in a monastery. 6

prehistoric (PREE-hih-STOHR-ik) — a time before history was recorded in writing. 4

reptiles (REHP-tylz) — cold-blooded animals that lay eggs and are covered with scales or plates. 18

scam (SCAM) — a lie. 10

Viking (VY-king) — Scandinavian seafarer or pirate who attacked Europe long ago. 6

INDEX